JUDGE ME, WRONG

ANGIE B.

Finding Truth Through Life Defining
Moments Right in Front of Your Face

ISBN: 978-0-692-16286-6

Library of Congress Cataloging-in-Publication Data has been applied for. Editors: P31 Publishing, LLC

For more information, please visit www.judgemewrong.com

Instagram: helloangieb

Dedication

I dedicate this book to self-doubt, discouragement, depression, suffering, anger, anxiety, sadness and fear. I welcome confidence, wisdom, peace, healing, forgiveness, standing up, discipline, and love, with open arms.

Contents

"Long live the rose that grew from concrete when no one else cared."

~Tupac Shakur

Introduction

This book is only the mere beginning of a conversation about many issues and topics that society prefer not to discuss. I consider this book to be one of my most valuable and precious gifts. Just so you know, you are embarking on a remarkable journey. As you read this book, I have one request, which is that you read this book with an open mind. We, tend to judge constantly, whether it's judging a person by their looks, past experiences, economic status, or just to get a laugh in. Judging a person can be detrimental no matter how you think or feel about it. Although, *Judge Me, Wrong,* will not stop others from judging a person, instead it will give one the in-depth on how to encourage yourself and others that, this thing called "life," shouldn't be a battlefield and we should never prejudge as we all have a story. We all have the power to overcome adversity and being resilient. *Judge Me, Wrong,* will make you laugh, it may make you cry, but most of all it will give you hope.

Angie B.

CHAPTER 1:

Four Leaf Clover

> *"There are two great days in a person's life — the day we are born and the day we discover why" ~ Mark Twain*

*P*ecan trees swayed gently in the wind while the oak trees were shedding their leaves, the robin birds were out chirping as you enjoyed the cool breeze against your skin. There was not a rain drop in sight, despite the thunder storm held just forty-eight hours ago. The only buckets of water were from Ann- tears of joy. There was something so special about this day, something was special about this baby, but Ann couldn't figure out what it was. Maybe it was the hours and hours of labor she was in. Ann was in labor 22 hours and the baby arrived two days early.

"Here you go Ann- a healthy baby girl! Do you have a name picked out?" the nurse asked, as she handed the wrapped up 6lb 6oz newborn to Ann. Ann looked down at her as she thought; this was her last and final child since she had just signed the papers to have a tubal ligation. Ann cradled the baby gently while gazing at her beautiful brown skin, and her beautiful hair. Ann and her baby bonded as they stared into each other eyes, Ann said, "Rose. Yes, Rose Baccara Scott."

"Oh. Ok. But if you don't mind me asking, what is the meaning behind her middle name?" the nurse asked. Ann replied, "Black Rose."

"Beautiful, simply beautiful!" the nurse smiled as she walked away.

Rose had no idea that her life would be all of any turmoil or would she become a statistic, a little brown girl growing up in an abusive single parent home. Would she become a product of her environment, or would she bloom into a beautiful Rose?

CHAPTER 2:

Tranquility Of Solitude

"Without great solitude no serious work is possible" ~ *Pablo Picasso*

As a young child Rose knew she was indifferent. She was very distant and always to herself. Growing up, Rose knew her mom as they were close- not close in hugs and kisses, but close. Ann was a single parent raising Rose and always kept Rose near her-sometimes a little overbearing, and extremely overprotective of Rose.

Rose's childhood was somewhat normal. She was a very sweet and polite child who was an A/B student throughout her school years. She always did as she was told- "Sit up straight, chew with your mouth closed, don't talk so loud." As the saying was, girls are supposed to be seen and not heard. She had a few family members that loved her and she always had a hot meal and a warm bed. But Rose was empty inside. You see, Rose never knew exactly who she was. Rose was ashamed and embarrassed. Embarrassed of the Department Agriculture Food Coupons that she would have to use to purchase food every month. Ashamed that she walked to school while all the other kids had parents to drop them off in the front on the curb. Jealous that she did not have her father there to call Daddy and lonely that she only spent time with her brothers and sisters every other week. Rose and her siblings had different fathers and the court system decided how they should live their lives. If you guessed, you're correct- Joint Custody. See reader, this wouldn't affect some, but it made a terrible impact with Rose. Being the youngest of five kids she felt alone even in a room full of people. Now what do you do when you are alone? You adapt, you become accustomed and begin to enjoy the perks of being in great solitude. It just seemed that anyone and almost everyone that she would get close to would always disappear, so being withdrawn and lonely became the norm for Rose.

At times, too much alone time is overbearing and not good socially. Ok; therefore you make yourself hang out with others, although it's cool and other times a little awkward. Just going with the flow.

So, there they were, Rose's neighborhood and "close friends." You know- the ones that will take you out of isolation. It was a group of them from the neighborhood- Rose, Brandon, Chris, Ashley, Brittany and sometimes Kevin would come around, but he wasn't sure if he was ready to come out the closet. Everyone knew he had a little sugar in his tank- so what, they didn't care. They all attended the same school and were in the same grade. It was quite natural they all congregatd together.

Kevin and Rose had the same personality; some would call it "anti-social" however, it was more like "anti-bullshit." Consequently, they hung when they felt like socializing and having small talk. Who cared they were different. They would ride their bikes or walk to the store and get any and everything they could buy with the money they put together. Either way, no one was walking out of the Mini-Mart without that Clearly Canadian flavored water that looked like wine coolers. Oh, did I just go there! I'm sure I did. If you grew up in the '90s then you know what I'm talking about. Ok, Ok, back to the story. There they were, sitting on whoever's porch that day with their snacks, while dancing and listening to TLC – "Ain't 2 Proud to Beg"- and if Jennifer and Ashley were around, they blasted, "Rhythm is a Dancer" by Snap. Now, Jennifer and Ashley were different- and you knew it. Ashley had long curly red hair and Jennifer had freckles on her cheek and nose. Jennifer's parents didn't really approve of her hanging with some of them and one day it was proven while Rose was over at her house. Her mom looked into her pupils with her blue eyes coming from her lenses and said, "Hey, Rose, you know you are welcome to come over anytime, you're not like, "them." "THEM!"she said, confused. "Oh, OK, Yes, Ma'am, Thank you!" Rose's lips managed to say, but her facial expression surely saying something else. She thought, what does that mean? Is it what I think it means? I'm accepted, yeah- what a compliment, right?! Still thinking in silence, she asked herself, this is what I want? To be accepted, to please people? Well, if I don't go over there and play with Jessica, will I miss her? Is it worth it? "Even though you look like them, you don't act like them." That conversation was like Rose had set it on repeat and as she walked home, she heard it over and over again. "Whatever!" she said out loud. Despite the shyness and reserve, contrary to the look, she was still one of "them." Never mind, I don't want the acceptance- I'd rather be alone."

CHAPTER 3:

In This Skin

"Dark skin is not a crime & light skin is not a prize"
~ *Urban Rogue*

"Oh, hey you're pretty for a dark skin girl." They would say…and then you think to yourself… Here we go again, how many times will a person say that- like come on give me a break already! Imagine that, always having to hear, 'stay out the sun you don't want to get black' or 'do you know who you remind me of, oh I know'… I'm sure it's someone of the same complexion. Wait, get this one- 'I don't date dark skin' and 'the darker the berry the sweeter the juice'. Um, excuse me, but what does that even mean? It makes you start to wonder why the Lord made you dark. It's just annoying. But those were the words Rose would hear quite often. Now get this, we are in century 21, and you have celebrities and Caucasian, Latinos, and even some Black women that are actually paying and going through high measures to tan their skin, get butt implants and even lip injections. Well, Rose hated everything about her brown-eyes, black skin, her excessively big lips, her nappy hair and her skinny body.

Then it was all proven why she didn't like her skin, that maybe what she was thinking was exactly how she was feeling. It was in grade school and it was the Christmas Program. Rose was to perform with DaShawn. They were to loop their arms together and dance. DaShawn was darker than she, with big teeth that would always have white saliva at the corners of his mouth. Gross! I know, right-but it's true. So, there they were; the time had come for them to perform in front of the teachers, administrators, their peers, family and friends. Well, as soon as the dance was over, DaShawn took his right hand and whipped his left arm and then folded his arms over his chest right there on stage. He did that in front of everyone. Rose was so embarrassed. He didn't do that as to say ewwww, girls have cooties, he did that because she was dark, skinny and in his eyes, ugly. Not ugly because of facial features but ugly because she was darker than anyone else, he looked at her as unpretty and she knew it- or that's how she felt. He had been complaining and griping for the past four weeks they had to rehearse. But she didn't want to dance with him either; even behind his back she talked to the teacher and asked if she could do something else. But the teacher claimed that there weren't any other parts and this was a major grade. Her feelings were hurt, she was crushed. She shut down and never spoke to him again. The school was very diverse, but until this day Rose still doesn't understand why the teacher paired them together.

On another occasion, while still in grade school, Rose was chosen for a paper that she had written, to recognize a student for a job well done on your accomplishment. They took your picture, and placed it on the bulletin board in the front located by the office for everyone to see. Ann made sure Rose had a new outfit and she got her hair done. Rose settled for braids and had the beautician put the beads on the end. Her hair was beautiful; she was cute. Well, someone didn't think so, because her picture was up there- along with everyone else that had great accomplishments in the course of those 6 weeks. Someone had the audacity to scratch out her lips on the picture. She was devastated and hurt. Rose thought, "Yes maybe my lips are too big, and that's why they scratched it off." But she didn't complain to anyone at the school.

When she walked in the house that day, Ann looked at her and questioned, "What's wrong?" Rose told her. Ann replied, "But you are black, with big teeth and lips." Rose's eyes grew big and watery as she looked at her mom thinking, 'that's not what you should say. Her lips began to tremble, and she ran into her room and cried herself to sleep. There wasn't anything that could be done. Ann had just validated the truth because she didn't lie. It was the skin she was born in and one day she would hopefully learn to embrace it.

CHAPTER 4:

Olive Branch

> *"Let no man pull you low enough to hate him."* ~Dr. Martin
> Luther King, Jr.

As the seasons starting changing, so did the relationship between Ann and Rose- especially Rose. Rose became bitter, she felt alone, miserable and confused. Rose was angry with her mother, despised her father, annoyed and disinterested with her older sisters and brothers; she felt hopeless and pessimistic. Ann was also angry, and she started taking her anger out on Rose. If you ever heard that saying, you hurt the ones that are closest to you- that's a proven fact. After countless days and months of physical, emotional and verbal abuse, Rose decided to run away from home. The first time she ran away, she ran to her older sister's home. This was one of her older sisters who lived the closet. The other sister was 500 miles away doing who knows what. Anyway, that was a bad idea. Her situation went from bad to worse; Rose had no choice but to go back home. For months, everything seemed like it was back to normal, but when Ann became outraged, she was like a volcanic eruption. After running away this time, Rose chose to go to her grandparent's home. They were more understanding, and they actually had no idea. After getting them involved, they involved Child Protective Services (CPS). Ann and Rose were assigned to complete therapy sessions, together and alone. After sitting countless hours in therapy, Ann thought it would be a good idea and time for Rose to meet her father.

Eye-to-eye, there he was, standing and staring at her like the man in the mirror after all those years. Deuces, that was him. Deuces was his street name, but his government name was Theopolis Lafayette. The story I hear about how he got that name was in his teen years, how he never stayed in the, same area longer than 15 minutes, and when you looked again he was gone, giving everyone the Deuces. Although he wasn't hard to find and he wasn't hiding either, it was now a bittersweet moment for Rose to now be able to see him in person rather that a picture. He walked up, dark shades, tears running down his cheek with his arms spread out wide, offering her an olive branch. Rose swallowed her pride and accepted – but she really just wanted to slap him in his face with it, turn around and walk off. Instead she embraced him, and listened to all of the 'you're so big, I miss you! I was coming to see you, just been working.' Rose's father-and the past, present and future lies he was telling? From his lips, through her left ear, and out her right.

Deuces had a family; well, he had his family and a common law wife who had five kids, three of them still living at home. That summer, Deuces took Rose around to meet her other siblings who welcomed her with open arms, but the same can't be said about his common law wife, Linda. At times, Linda had a welcoming spirit with excellent hospitality and other times she was cantankerous and cunning. Rose didn't stay long that summer. After leaving, she wouldn't see her father for another 15 years.

CHAPTER 5:

Teenage Euphoria

"Pessimism is your friend, Euphoria the enemy."
Warren Buffett

*E*very channel you turned to there it was, the infamous white Ford Bronco pursuit and the US being divided yet again by race- "HE DID IT"/ "NO, HE'S INNOCENT UNTIL PROVEN GUILTY." But that TV broadcast of news was nothing of Rose's concern. She didn't care about the Heisman or the "Juice" or anything CNN or BET were broadcasting as "breaking news." She considered herself to be floating on Cloud 9. She was excited because she had a steady boyfriend like all her other friends. This is what some would call a teenage love affair-yeah I guess so. That didn't matter to Rose; she was just excited that someone she went to school with called her pretty, walked her to class, and showed her undeniable attention. Jungle was one year older than Rose, and very charming and sweet. Jungle was the type of guy to write a two-page letter professing his feelings and love. He would walk her to her class and hold her books. This is everything Rose had dreamed of, since all of her friends had steady boyfriends and were in relationships, some even older with cars. Rose fell madly in love- or maybe it was infatuation since she was so young and naive. All summer, Rose and Jungle spent all of their time together. Maybe a little bit too much time. Because as the school year was fast approaching' Jungle became distant from Rose and this was the beginning of a new season.

Wednesday, September 6, 1995, the first day of Rose's junior year and Jungle's senior year at Hidden Hills High. Everything seemed to be ok between Rose and Jungle. But then the late night calls became minimal, he was no longer waiting for her at the end of the class period when the bell rang. Jungle even stopped writing letters.

Rose was walking down the hall heading to 4th period. "Hey Rose- wait up!," Kevin screeched.

"Hey Kevin, what's popping!" Rose said.

Kevin started, "Gurrrrllll, I ain't the one to gossip so you ain't heard this from me, but yo' boy Jungle is playing you."

Nah, Kev, you tripping," Rose said "How can he? He spends all his time with me. We're always together; how can he play me?"

"I don't know, just check yo' boy," Kevin said. Kevin and Rose walked to class and sat down in their seats waiting for roll call. That day Rose didn't see Jungle because he skipped that day and was upset with Rose for not skipping with him.

Later that night, Rose's cousin called her on the phone to tell her she heard Jungle was talking to Brittany and saw him walking her to class and hanging by the lockers. Things started to add up and make sense for Rose because Jungle never had time for her anymore or when she paged him he didn't call back. After about 2 months had passed and all the snickering and talk behind Rose's back, Jungle finally came out and told Rose he needed some space. Rose went into a deep depression because now something was growing inside of her stomach and she wasn't sure what was going on. The only person that truly knew everything was her girl and neighbor Ashley who she confided in. Ashley had just dropped out of high school last year because she was a teen mom. Now, Rose had started to believe she would be following down the same path. "NO! This can't be happening!" Rose cried as she told Ashley. "I'm late with my cycle. I don't know how to tell my mom and when I tell her she will kill me!"

As days went by, Rose was thinking of strategies and home remedies on how to have a miscarriage. That's the only thing she was thinking about- how to get rid of what was growing inside of her. Rose would pick up furniture, move it around, run up and down the stairs. Nothing seemed to work and now the father of her baby was no longer speaking and wanting to be with her.

Jungle was acting as though she didn't exist. One day Rose passed right by Jungle in the hallway and Jungle walked on by, nonchalant and had the audacity to call her that night.

"Hey! We need space," he said.

Rose didn't reply verbally, she just stood there confused.

"Look," he said. "I don't want to be with you; I usually don't date dark skin girls. I only date, "light complexion females." Their conversation was going nowhere.

"Save the chitter chat!" Rose finally managed to say and hung up. The thunderstorm poured from her eyes. She was devastated. Now, Jungle did make it a pattern to be with other girls and taunt it in her face and yes, they were all light skinned. He would showboat and prance all in front of her. It was talk all around the school how he was acting like he never knew her, and all the while Rose still had something she believed to be a baby growing inside.

CHAPTER 6:

Tears For An Unplanned Pregnancy

"She was brought into this world out of a beautiful mistake when her mom was just a girl and her daddy didn't stay." ~ *Author Unknown*

Clear Blue, e.p.t., and First Response- all of them positive. Two pink lines. Wait, let me do again! Two pink lines. The results were not changing- am I in denial? Now, I am asking myself and trying to understand the resolution of taking the test when I can clearly feel something inside my womb, Rose thought. The only thing to do now is hide it, right? Rose began to wear bigger clothing and jackets to hide her growing stomach. Rose felt like that 10 year-old girl who was alone. Rose didn't know how far along she was because she hadn't been to a doctor. She did know that Jungle was enjoying his senior year- dating and courting different girls, smiling and laughing in Rose's face. Rose knew everyone was talking behind her back because she was simply alone and everyone turned their nose up to her.

See, in the year 1995 you dare not have a baby while in high school, or anytime being unmarried and uneducated.

Pregnant girls were segregated from the others; they were not allowed to be with the regular population. During the late '90s and early 2000s once you became pregnant you were sent to another school. I guess you can call it the "pregnant girl's school." But Rose didn't want to be labeled and hid her pregnancy from everyone. "Where are you hiding that baby?" They would ask Rose, or "how did you hide your pregnancy from everyone?" Rose would always explain that "It wasn't easy." She would then go on to explain that, she wore big- baggy shirts and pants and always had on a light windbreaker for at least 6 months. Rose had to let go of all her stylish clothing- her one favorite outfit was with the blue denim Nike skirts and Nike t-shirts you would tuck in. Now keep in mind, Rose only weighed 97 lbs. Yep, size 0. Rose didn't have a chance to enjoy her pregnancy or have a baby shower.

Ann didn't find out about Rose's pregnancy until Rose was in her last trimester. She hid that baby bump to the end. Ann was distraught like any mother would be, but also like any mother she cared and loved Rose unconditionally.

"NOOOOOO ROSE! SSTOPPPPPPPP! DON'T YOU HAVE THAT BABY IN THE TOILET! CALL 911!"

Ann frantically screamed, but Rose was in excruciating pain. There they were, the sirens and all the flashing lights. The nurse is screaming, "DON'T PUSH!"

"I CAN'T HOLD IT," Rose squealed back, the pain and contractions more powerful than the last. This is overwhelming, Rose thought. She was exposed, and her main source of support had been admitted. Ann- she was now in her own hospital bed- she couldn't take it!

After careful consideration and Ann giving Rose the OK. she had made the decision not to put her baby up for adoption, but being a teen mom, finishing high school and working part-time was a challenge. Sometimes, in life we make sudden decisions under pressure and some decisions will make an impact, at times good or bad. However, once you make the decision you have to also make the decision to live with it. Rose, was covered in stress- financial stress, baby blues, socially deprived, and babysitting issues just to name a few.

As Rose laid in bed, listening to Lauryn Hill's CD The Miseducation of Lauryn Hill, she starting thinking. Does she raise this kid on her own? Can she do it by herself? Will she be able to let go of the only guy she shared her heart with? I'm sure we all have been in this type of situation. How do you let go? How will you ever get over it? Well like the old folk say, keep waking up and saying good morning. Does she let go and walk away from this guy, her daughter's father, or does she stay? As Rose struggled with this, letting go, her phone rang, and it was him, Jungle. Jungle called to say they needed space. Because of course it was an off again on again relationship. There's the sign! Rose thought. I guess Jungle had found someone else so he was ready to be over. Rose thought as Lauryn sang, "When it hurts so bad," How much effort can a person put into trying to salvage a teenage love affair?

Days turned into weeks, weeks into months before she would hear from Jungle. Rose's Prime-Co phone went off. It was Jungle. "Hey!" Rose said.

"MAN," "WHAT'S THIS PAPER I GOT." Jungle screamed through the phone.

"I need you to lower your tone," Rose said.

"MAN LOOK I DON'T HAVE TO PLAY GAMES WITH YOU. SO YOU PUTTING CHILD SUPPORT ON ME?" Jungle continued to scream.

"Whatever, Jungle. I don't have time for this."

"I TOLD YOU I WOULD HELP YOU WITH DAY-CARE AND I'LL GIVE IT TO YOU, WHEN I GIVE IT TO YOU!"

"Look, the baby is crying, I got to go." Rose said, then she hung up; and as typical, Jungle called back. "Why did you hang up?"

"I told you Beauty is crying, and I need to take care of her," Rose said.

"Well we need to talk so call me back when you're done."

Jungle constantly called Rose's phone all night. Rose had just put Beauty down for her nap. It was a beautiful Saturday evening and Rose had planned to study to prepare for the SAT test today. As Rose sat on the porch with her bare feet on the concrete drinking her lemonade tea she started to question herself. Why was she going through so much at an early age? Will she be able to forgive those that betrayed her or hurt her the most? Why was she going through so much pain?

It is a fantasy to believe that we as humans will go through life and not experience pain. Although, no one wants the pain, it can't always be so easy.

Rose thought, so it is true- having a baby will make a man stay. Maybe it was proof because now Jungle wanted to be with Rose. There it goes again. Maybe this is exactly what Rose wanted. Did she really get pregnant or purpose to keep Jungle? Did she really love him or was it a pure accident between two inexperienced teenage kids? Well, she had no time to contemplate and inquire about the what-ifs; she had to live with the consequence of her choice. The damage has already been done. Jungle and Rose began to date again. Yes, of course, you read that right; they were back on and everything was still on Jungle's terms. Jungle was sending Rose through an emotional rollercoaster. One minute he was down, the next day they were over. It was just too much of back and forth, and Rose wanted more. She and Beauty deserved better. Rose needed Jungle to support more financially and actually be there for their baby. Jungle had now graduated from high school and he was beginning to turn into a "Toys R Us kid." He still wasn't working and staying home with his parents. Rose was going to school full time and working as a telemarketer part-time. Jungle wasn't assisting her financially at all and their relationship was suddenly declining. Jungle never had time for Rose or Beauty. Then it started again, the cheating. Jungle turned into a different person towards Rose. Whenever she would ask him for financial assistance, he would turn into a screaming lunatic.

Tears have become Rose's best friend.

CHAPTER 7:

Mirror And Darkest Shades

"You don't know pain until you're staring at yourself in the mirror with tears in your eyes, begging yourself to just hold on and be strong." ~Word Porn

*A*lthough tears have become Rose's best friend and confidant, one must understand that tears express both delight and grief.

Have you ever looked in the mirror and not liking the image of what you have become?

That is exactly how Rose was feeling, along with solitude- not because she wanted to be alone, but alone because she had no choice. Rose wasn't able to hang out with her friends, most of them no longer her friend, the daycare bill was steadily escalating. Beauty required more time and attention. Her manager at her job was not understanding, and she had a seven-page report due for school. When you sit down and think about it, it's a lot for a young teen to go through. Where was everyone that said they would help?

Where was everyone that said; I can and will babysit anytime you need me- call me if you need me, if you need anything just let me know? But no one was answering their phones, or they had plans. Where was everyone, when you needed them the most?

Rose stood in front as the reflection stared back. She was hurting after holding all of the pain inside. At that moment, it seemed as though her self-image was telling her to stand up for herself and fight. As Rose took off her shades she made up her mind to not hide anymore; she was taking back her soul. Allowing the mirror to expose her true beauty, strengths and weakness, she said to herself, you will get through this, you can overcome it, be strong for yourself and your baby girl.

CHAPTER 8:

Every Rose Has Its Thorns

> *"If eyes can define the soul, as windows do the world. Through you I see, joy and pain through deep and black pearls."*
> ~ *Angie B.*

"Is this guy following me?" Rose had seen the same guy a few times-this was the third time Rose saw this guy. It appeared that he knew her; as Rose walked through the store she could see someone was watching and following her. So, she went the other way, she was a little frightened. But there he was again; you couldn't see his eyes or his face. He was dressed in all black with a hat so low his eyes were not revealed.

"Hello, let me get that for you," he said.

"Sure," Rose said, as he held the door.

"What is your name?" the man in black asked.

"Rose," she said.

"Hello, Rose," L.A., the man in black said, extending his hand. "Nice to meet."

Rose and L.A. dated a few months and their relationship was growing stronger although both of them were mentally not ready for a steady relationship. They both had just gotten out of relationships that were full of lies, deceit and heartbreak, to name a few. The relationship was refreshing- L.A. was charming, but what she adored most was his veracity. L.A. had two sons from a previous relationship and Rose had Beauty. The two kids bonded very quickly and nicely. As they bonded and blended as a family, it started to expand and multiply. L.A. and Rose had a child together, a boy. Although they remained unmarried, this time the father of the child was there.

A few years went by and then one day, Rose felt weird. She knew the feeling all too well, she had she went through it when she was only a teen..

Rose called her boyfriend, L.A. and told him how she was feeling and the results. He reassured her that whatever decision she wanted to make he would support her. That night, Rose had decided. and by the next morning Rose would be sitting in the doctor's office.

There they were again, all the protesters with signs that read STOP ABORTION NOW, BABIES ARE MURDERED HERE, YOU ARE GOING TO HELL. Rose threw on a cap, scarf and her Ray- Bans and she walked into the clinic.

Rose's thoughts were racing. This cannot be happening again. There L.A. was, calm. "Whatever you want to do, I got you," he said. It was always left to Rose to make the decision. "It's your body." Yes, it was, but this was killing Rose softly- mentally, killing Rose softly. She felt extreme depression and mood swings.

After completing all the consent forms and reviewing HIPPA and answering numerous questions, the dark- haired nurse finally said, "OK, I see you're here for a D & E" -a slight way of saying, "abortion." But Rose was so far along, that she would be back at the clinic the next two days for the two- part procedure. Day one- prep and take pill to stop the pregnancy and day two – surgical procedure. Then there was the nurse with the usual questions. Do you have any kids? How many? Marital status, health information, blah, blah, blah... All the questions that get all in your private business. The procedure took less than an hour. Once the procedure was over, they brought Rose into the recovery room.

Back at the house, L.A. was very nurturing. He helped Rose into bed, making sure she had taken her medication and reassuring her that everything was going to be OK. As Rose lay there, she wasn't sure how to feel. Will God punish her? Will he forgive her? Did she make the right decision?

It's OK!1... - "You had to do it!" But why did she have to do it? Either way she tried to reassure herself with every rationale possible. "Another mouth to feed!" "You're not married yet!"

Please don't confuse the morning after with the abortion pill. It's not the same. This time she was able to choose the morning after pill; she was 2 weeks pregnant. Some may wonder why she just didn't get on birth control to avoid this. Well with life, you can't explain everything.

CHAPTER 9:

No White Flag - Never Give Up

"Winners never quit, and quitters never win."
~*Vince Lombardi*

TEN, NINE, EIGHT, SEVEN, SIX, FIVE, FOUR, THREE, TWO, ONE- HAPPY NEW YEAR!

New Year, New Beginnings – the cleansing has begun.

With a New Year is a new beginning. The time has come, actually it's overdue.

With a New Year comes a new fresh start. Rose believe, there are two times for a new year. The New Year when we change the number and our birthday year. Just like everyday when we go from sunrise to sunset is a new beginning. With time, comes change and sometimes the evolution of change is overdue. We spend a lot of out time dwelling on the past and beating ourselves up instead of growing and manifesting. Often times we dont give ourselves enough credit and downplay our self-worth. We tend to dismiss our ability of growth and allowing ourselves to make mistakes and learn from them, when it's part of the development and growing process. Sometimes we even allow people to bring up our past mistakes, allowing them to speak negatively and stating things like I remember when; you were this way or when you did this. Although, we graduated from that hurtful position and turmoil in our lives. There are still folks out there who is waiting to bring it up. That's why it is imperative that we must first accept and love ourselves, two, know our self worth and three Believe. Always believe in thyself. Believe! Believe! Believe! I must admit, I didn't believe in myself. I had made a mistake of getting pregnant at the young age of sixteen. They said, she will become a product of her environment. She will have babies after babies, living and depending on the system. She will not graduate, She Did! She will not go to college. She Did! She won't get far in life, she has! And it's all because she believed in herself. She ran the race and finished the course and at the the finish line she threw away the self doubt, the shame, and insecurities and she embraced self discovery and self-love.

Now the Bloom

You've heard Rose's story and the things that happened in her life. You many even think ell, thats been done before. Yes, you may be right. She wasn't the first and she will not be the last. More often than not that's not the case for everyone. Unfortunately, some pre-teens to young adults come out stronger than ever and some struggle. When I speak of struggle, I'm speaking suicide, depression, incarceration and physical/mental abuse relationships. Some may even follow the pattern of having more children and it becomes an unbreakable cycle. Some may even have a more pain or painful experience, but whatever it is, a lot of us are fighting our own battles. Regardless, if it's anxiety, low self-esteem, and peer pressure. Whatever it is, just know that you are not alone, we all need healing. Life is a process of growing, outgrowing, growing some more and being reborn. Again, you must know your worth. I've had and still have many special and important people in my life, some are still alive and I talk and text on a daily basis. Some who hold a special spot in my heart because they or no longer with me but taught me some valuable lessons. That is, what life is about, Lessons. One in particular is "You are Valuable!" Now, I've had and have life coaches/mentors, but one I've come along way under her tutelage, and she would always say, 'YOU MUST STAND FOR SOMETHING OR YOU WILL FOR ANYTHING", you see reader, I have that in all caps because she wouldn't be screaming at me, she would just turn the volume up a little because she, was so passionate and seh believed in me and didn't want me to just settle. So, Reader, I'm telling you, "STAND FOR SOMETHING, DO NOT FALL FOR ANYTHING,"

You have survive thus far, and you will continue to survive. Stop questioning and second guessing yourselves and asking if you are good enough, because you are, we are! Don't give them the white flag!

The moral of the story, plain as the eyes can see…. Rose is I and I am She'

I thank God for allowing me to go to through the many storms I went through and always covering and protecting me to be able to share my thorns with you. Always remember that no matter how dark the forecast, every cloud has a silver lining.

Peace and Blessings - *Angie B' (Rose)*

Acknowledgements

If you are at the end and still holding & finish reading this book - Big Ups, I appreciate it. Big Thanks to my wonderful mother, who is my biggest inspiration. I didn't understand then, but I understand now and as you would always say, what is understood, doesn't have to be explained. Nathaniel Smith, for giving me my first urban book. I remember it so vividly. We were at Ma house and I said I was tired of reading, "those," encyclopedias, I mean come on, the encyclopedia was educational but BORING, I needed a new genre. Believe, me you gave me a book filled with lots of twists and turns, WOW it was full of drama. I'm here to say, that is when I fell in love with reading and writing. My hat goes off to you. Bottoms up to my wonderful husband, Big E. Thanks for believing in me and my vision and all the love and support. You are the real MVP, you dig! My amazeball kids, you are definitely my pride and joy and you bring me so much happiness. You all are my favorites. No, seriously, the both of you are the Greatest Of All Times and it will make me even happier if you wouldn't use up all the toilet paper. To my bonus son, I appreciate your kindness and respect most of all. Bubba, you are one of a kind, you are greatly appreciated. Toya, you're the best! You started writing first and published your book, you pumped me up…. I can hear you now saying, Angie! Listen! Girl! you can do it and you sound so much like Aunt Ronnie. Thanks for everything, I truly appreciate it. Much love to all of my guardian angels above. To my wonderful editor, publisher and team. I don't know how many times I went back and forth with this editing but we made it through. Jasmine, your professionalism is out of sight! Me mentor, Shawn T. I'm just going to say, "BOOM" and leave it at that! Much love to all the mothers, fathers, siblings and family members who have found their way.

Wait! You didn't think I would forget about _____. How could I?! Thank You, _____, for all that you've done and continue to do. OMG! _____ thanks for being you and never change, _____ you have a heart of gold and are simply beautiful inside and out. _____ thank you, you didn't even know that I was your protege all them years, I appreciate your wisdom and guidance, and it shall always be death before dishonor, so stay loyal my friend. Thank you to _____ for your wonderful hospitality, and _____, and _____ and _____. You guys are amazing and like they say in Texas, Allllllready!

10 Rose Petal Questions to Discuss

Rose Petal 1 - Was there ever a time in your life when you felt like everyone was misjudging you?

_____

_____

_____

How did that make you feel and what did you do?

_____

_____

_____

Rose Petal 2 - Do you have weakness(s) and what are you doing to turn them into a strength?

_____

_____

_____

Rose Petal 3 - Do you think families should withhold family secrets? Do you believe in the myth of? "What goes on in my house, stays in my house?"

_____

_____

_____

Rose Petal 4 - What would you do as a mother if your teen got pregnant? What if she wanted to keep the baby? Would you let her? What if it was your son, that impregnated a girl? What would you do?

_____

_____

_____

Rose Petal 5 - Do you support Planned ParentHood? What are your thoughts with women rights and fertility?

_____

_____

_____

Rose Petal 6 - Do you have any ill will or resentment from your past? Why? Do you think you can forgive that person(s)?

_____

_____

_____

Rose Petal 7 - Do you think fathers are crucial in a girls life?

_____

_____

_____

Rose Petal 8 - Are your living in your truth?

_____

_____

_____

Rose Petal 9 - Are you honest with yourself?

_____

_____

_____

Rose Petal 10 - Would you recommend this book?

_____

_____

_____